Original title:
Lily's Lament

Copyright © 2025 Creative Arts Management OÜ
All rights reserved.

Author: Beckett Sinclair
ISBN HARDBACK: 978-1-80566-659-2
ISBN PAPERBACK: 978-1-80566-944-9

Echoes of an Untold Farewell

In the garden, whispers roam,
With petals swirling, far from home.
A gnome with issues of great flight,
   Winks at shadows in the night.

Frogs croak tales of yesteryears,
While squirrels dance, ignoring fears.
A snail slips past with a wink and grin,
   Chasing secrets blown by wind.

The flowers giggle, petals pink,
As they ponder what to think.
An old bee buzzes, rather slow,
And trips on pollen, steals the show.

As laughter lingers through the leaves,
   A tiny ant plays tricks, deceives.
   In this realm where jesters play,
   Goodbyes are merely games today.

The Gentle Fall of Evening Light

As dusk descends, the crickets cheer,
They serenade all who draw near.
The sun takes bows, then starts to snooze,
While broomsticks dance in evening's hues.

A ladybug in polka dots,
Orders snacks from the teapot.
With giggles soft, and more to share,
The night unfolds its funny flair.

A bunny juggles clover heads,
While whispers bloom in flowerbeds.
The stars above begin to snicker,
As night's delights grow ever thicker.

In shadows cast by moon's embrace,
A firefly contests with grace.
And as the soft light starts to play,
Laughter brightens up the way.

The Garden's Hidden Sorrows

Beneath the leaves, a tale unfolds,
Of squash that dreamed of being bold.
A worm with flair is quite the catch,
Yet he can't seem to find a match.

The daisies pout in sunny rows,
They envy the gleam of the snappy rose.
A hedgehog sighs, his spines a mess,
He wishes he could wear a dress.

But laughter lingers through the vines,
With secrets stitched in garden lines.
A crow caws jokes, no one can tease,
As flowers laugh and bend their knees.

And when the moon casts silver light,
The garden giggles, full of delight.
For in their hearts, they know too well,
That in the funny, sorrows dwell.

Reflections in the Moonlit Water

A pond reflects a winking moon,
Where frogs croak silly, merry tunes.
The fishes splash with giddy glee,
As ripples dance like poetry.

The reeds stand tall, they shake and sway,
They've got some gossip too, to say.
A turtle dons a top hat bright,
While minnows dip for sheer delight.

In silver beams, the laughter flows,
Casting shadows that strike a pose.
A dragonfly flaunts its wings at night,
Thinking it's quite the dazzling sight.

And as the water giggles low,
The moon grins wide, to steal the show.
In every wave, the joy anew,
Reflects the fun that's always true.

A Journey Through Heavy Clouds

In skies of gray, the sun did hide,
A flower's quest, a humorous ride.
With raindrops drumming on her head,
She danced like mad, while others fled.

Through puddles deep and mud so thick,
She slipped and slid, a funny trick.
Her petals soggy, yet she grinned,
For laughter's warmth was how she'd win.

A cloud burst forth, a sudden shout,
"Why didn't you just take a route?"
But off she went, a splashing spree,
This silly flower, wild and free.

In stormy realms, she found her gum,
A squeaky laugh, a soggy drum.
With all her joy, she rode the rain,
A cheerful bud, through gray, insane.

Fraying Threads of a Garden's Tale

In twilight glow, the colors fade,
A tangle of yarn, a grand parade.
Petals pulled, a stitch undone,
This garden's craft is quite the fun!

With gnomes that giggle, frogs that cheer,
They dangle jokes, winking near.
"Your garden's tangled! What a view!"
She laughed aloud, "Oh, yes, it's true!"

Threads of laughter weave so bright,
In patchy blooms, a comical sight.
She knotted joy in every strand,
A playful touch from clumsy hand.

Yet blooming wildly with no care,
Was she a flower, or a big square?
With frayed edges and colors bold,
A garden tale that never gets old.

Notes of a Sunlit Soliloquy

In beaming rays, she found her voice,
A flowery song, by chance, no choice.
"Why do we wilt? What's with the fuss?"
The bees just buzzed, "What's the big plus?"

With petals wide and stamen tall,
She serenaded, entertaining all.
"Come join my zest, let's dance and sway,
Forget your woes, come laugh today!"

Through sunny days and breezy nights,
She spun a tale, full of delights.
"Why do flowers always pout?"
They giggled loud, "You're what it's about!"

In harmony, they laughed with glee,
Under the sun, so wild and free.
With notes like laughter in the air,
A sunny soliloquy, without a care.

Garden of Shadows

In shaded nooks, where giggles creep,
A garden thrums, not quiet, deep.
With shadows playing hide and seek,
She wobbled by, a clumsy peak.

"I'm not a weed," she squeaked with glee,
"Just thriving here, can't you see?"
The cacti snickered, roots entwined,
"Stay funky, flower, keep us blind!"

Through twisted vines and leafy pranks,
She twirled around, avoiding thanks.
"I'm just a bloom, a little jest,
Living my life like all the rest!"

Beneath the moon, the laughter swells,
In shadowed glades, where whimsy dwells.
A garden bright, where jokes ignite,
In secret blooms, her joy takes flight.

The Veil of a Shimmering Past

In the garden where echoes play,
A sheep in shades of blue took sway.
It danced with glee, but lost its hat,
Now it's quite the fashionable brat.

A gentle breeze brings tales of yore,
Where daffodils had much to score.
Their gossip swirls like confetti bright,
A squeaky tale of pure delight.

Yet among the blooms, a bee will dash,
To steal the show, all in a flash.
With flower crowns, the insects cheer,
As petals fall, they have no fear.

So let us laugh beneath the trees,
Where sunshine spills like honeyed bees.
A shimmering past, so wild and free,
Is filled with quirks and jubilee.

Tears of the Sunlit Afternoon

In the sunny nook where shadows leap,
A squirrel steals a nap, not a peep.
As clouds drift by with laughter loud,
The sun just blushes, oh so proud.

Butterflies with wings like lace,
Decide to host a silly race.
Flipping through the grass with flair,
They lose their way without a care.

An owl snickers from a nearby tree,
"Oh look, a bumblebee in a spree!"
He puffs his cheeks, puts on a grin,
Claims daytime fun is a kind of sin.

But as time weaves its funny tale,
Laughter ripples, never pale.
Underneath the golden hue,
The world is bright, and so are you.

When Stillness Holds Its Breath

In stillness where the silence roams,
A cat pretends to chase its gnomes.
With every leap, the world stands still,
As if the air had lost its will.

A turtle shuffles, slow and grand,
While ants critique its marching band.
"Hey, pick it up! It's half past late!"
But all they find is tasty bait.

The sun hangs low, a laughing friend,
While shadows stretch, refusing to bend.
And with a wink, the breeze will say,
"Hold your breath, it's a funny day!"

Amid all this, the world will grin,
Each careful pause becomes a win.
So let us toast to humor bright,
When stillness dances with delight.

Remnants of the Wistful Tides

By the shore where whispers sing,
A clam's found wearing a shiny ring.
It struts with pride, a royal show,
As waves roll in, it steals the glow.

Seagulls squawk with feathered flair,
Critique the beachwear, oh so rare.
"Is that a shell or just a hat?"
And crabs join in, "We're all that!"

The tide pulls back, with giggles sweet,
Unveiling treasures at our feet.
A lost flip-flop makes hearts soar,
As laughter echoes from the shore.

So let's embrace the rising fun,
As ocean tales are spun and done.
With remnants scattered all around,
A jesting world, where joys abound.

Chasing Echoes in the Breeze

A flower once tried to dance,
But tripped on its own little pants.
The wind laughed with glee,
As petals flew free.

It chased after clouds, bright and round,
While giggling bees buzzed all around.
The sun winked above,
As if sharing love.

In hopes of a breeze, it took flight,
Spinning and swirling, what a sight!
But tangled in twine,
Said, "I'm out of line!"

Yet onward it swayed, without care,
For daisies rejoiced in the air.
Together, they spun,
In a dance full of fun.

The Final Dance of Petals

As petals prepare to depart,
They twirl with a laugh, full of heart.
A wind's playful shove,
Sent them soaring above.

"Let's dance," one petal did call,
While tripping and tumbling, they all fall.
With colors so bold,
It's a sight to behold.

They hopped to a tune made of air,
In pirouettes, full of flair.
Though some fell behind,
They just didn't mind!

So on they continued, with a grin,
Embracing the fun in the spin.
Each petal had flair,
As laughter filled air.

Where Dreams and Waters Meet

In a pond where reflections play,
A frog croaked out, "Hip Hip Hooray!"
The lilies did cheer,
With petals quite near.

They nestled in dreams of a swim,
While teasing the bugs on a whim.
"Watch me dive, I'm bold!"
Said the lily, quite old.

But the splash sent them swirling in fright,
As the frog laughed away in delight.
"Oh dear, what a mess!
This dancing's no less!"

So there, by the waters so bright,
They laughed at the splash, what a sight!
In their watery gleam,
They danced in a dream.

The Fading Whispers of Blossoms

In a garden where whispers are soft,
The flowers would giggle and scoff.
"Can you hear that sound?
It's my sweet love bound!"

But a breeze brushed by with a chuckle,
And caused quite a raucous, a shuffle.
With petals askew,
They all blurted, "Phew!"

Yet fluttering here and there,
Made everyone stop and stare.
"Are we fading away,
Or just here to play?"

With each passing breeze, they would sigh,
"Let's twirl, and forget time's sly lie."
Once bright blooms now hush,
As they dance in a rush.

Silence That Cradles the Night

In the moon's soft, silver glow,
Crickets chirp with quite the show.
A raccoon dances, full of glee,
Stealing snacks as bold as me.

Stars above with twinkling eyes,
Watch the mischief, hear the sighs.
Nighttime whispers tales so bright,
In a dreamy, playful flight.

In the Company of Fallen Leaves

Crunchy whispers underfoot,
Squirrels plotting in a suit.
Autumn makes the trees a clown,
A red disguise, a leafy crown.

Chasing shadows, leaves will flip,
Every gust a comical trip.
Nature giggles in the breeze,
As we dance with rustling trees.

Echoes of a Distant Dawn

Roosters crow in playful jest,
Rising sun, you are the best.
Chasing shadows, birds take flight,
Coffee brews, oh what a sight!

Cup in hand, we laugh and cheer,
Morning chaos, never fear.
Toasts are made with silly grins,
As the day, again, begins.

The Layered Sigh of Nature

Mountains giggle with each breeze,
Tickling valleys, bringing tease.
Rivers flow with jokes untold,
In every bend, new laughter bold.

Trees exchange their leafy pranks,
While rocks stand firm in stoic ranks.
Nature's chorus, bright and round,
Echoes joy in every sound.

Fading Embers of Time

Once I lost my sock, oh dear,
Its twin is now a lonely sphere.
Time flies by, as socks will do,
Like cheese that's tossed to hungry goo.

I looked in drawers and under beds,
The tale of socks, it fills with dreads.
Each hole is but a tiny plot,
A mystery wrapped in a dirty lot.

Yet laughter breaks the somber gloom,
When missing socks give rise to bloom.
In little things, we find the fun,
A jest with mates, the day is won.

So here's to time, both quick and slow,
And all the socks we'll never know.
Each time we lose, a smile will chime,
In fading embers of our time.

The Softness of Lost Moments

A muffin once sat on my plate,
I blinked, and now it met its fate.
In crumbs and giggles, we recall,
The sweetness lost, but not too tall.

A strict diet tried to intrude,
Yet soft moments just scream for food.
With every bite, a memory made,
In laughter shared, the calories fade.

Old loves were like the pies I baked,
They vanished fast, while I just faked.
Of sweetness swirled in every crust,
A soft reminder, it's all unjust.

We'll raise our forks and toast the jest,
For lost moments are never the best.
But in each bite, a joy will bloom,
A softness found in every room.

Traces of a Distant Song

The cat sings tunes from way up high,
As I sit back and watch it fly.
With tails and paws, they dance around,
Instead of me, it's purring sound.

Forgotten notes float through the air,
A chorus of hairballs and despair.
The melody's lost, but still it plays,
In silly yowls and kitty ballet.

I hum along to what I hear,
A tune of chaos and meowed cheer.
Each scratch and pounce, a note to claim,
In traces left, we play the game.

So let us dance in this strange fog,
With every humor, seize the log.
A distant song will always call,
In feline whimsy, we'll never fall.

A Heart Weighing Down the Pond

I dropped my sandwich in the lake,
The fish swam close, for goodness' sake!
I stared in awe as they all gawked,
My heart sank deep, but they just talked.

With each sad splash, my hopes did dive,
The bread that floated, oh, not alive!
It's not just lunch that's lost at sea,
But dreams of picnics under a tree.

Yet laughter ripples through the muck,
For moments gone are just bad luck.
In sips of tea, we'll share the plight,
Of soggy bread under moon's light.

So let the heart weigh down the pond,
With laughter brightening each big yawn.
For even sandwiches drift away,
And joyful puns are here to stay.

In the Garden of Forgotten Sighs

In the garden, flowers whisper low,
Each petal giggles, letting secrets flow.
The daisies tease the weary sun's face,
While roses pout, declaring their grace.

Bees buzz round, planning a parade,
Dancing in circles, hilariously displayed.
The violets chuckle, wearing a grin,
As laughter erupts from within the din.

A gnome stands guard with a silly hat,
Pondering life, oh, what's up with that?
Garden critters share sarcastic jests,
Even the weeds are wearing their vests.

So, join the fun in this flowered game,
In a world where laughter outshines the fame.
For in this plot, where blooms have cried,
Joy reigns supreme, let the folly abide.

Vanishing Vows

Promises made with a chuckle and cheer,
Like socks in the dryer, just disappear.
"I swear I'll be true," one chortles aloud,
As love tumbles awkwardly in front of a crowd.

Nuptials set in a circus-like flair,
Vows exchanged with a wink and a dare.
"Through thick and thin, I'll always be there,"
Until they run off with the neighbor's pet mare.

Champagne spills while the best man sings,
The bride's holding back a fit of sweet flings.
Dancing away from the cheeky surprise,
With laughter echoing, they improvise.

As wedding cakes tumble and laughter ignites,
Every moment's a joke, as love takes flight.
For what's love without giggles and glee?
Just a riddle wrapped in a mystery!

The Depths of Solitude

In a room full of socks, with a curious frog,
Loneliness croaks like an old, sleepy dog.
The curtains are too shy to dance in the breeze,
While dust bunnies host soirées with ease.

Books on the shelf all share sticky notes,
Whispering jokes while the introvert gloats.
Each corner filled with echoes grand,
Where shadows debate if they can stand.

A chair reclines, pretending it's wise,
And a clock ticks slowly, making us sigh.
But wait! Is that laughter from under the bed?
No, just an old sandwich that probably fled.

In this realm of chuckles and solitude's gift,
Every sigh certainly has a playful twist.
So pulse with the jokes that the silence imparts,
For loneliness is just laughter in parts.

Traces of a Gentle Grace

In a meadow where giggles take flight,
Soft whispers of elegance dance in the light.
A butterfly trips over its own pretty wings,
While daisies chuckle with the joy that it brings.

Each breeze that meanders is painted in fun,
As petals stir gently, saying, 'We've won!'
With each soft brush, they tickle the air,
While laughter emerges from everywhere.

A deer prances by with a skip in its leap,
"Have you heard the latest?" it quips with a peep.
Nature tunes in to a sweet serenade,
While trees murmur secrets, their branches displayed.

So follow the traces of gentle allure,
Where humor and kindness forever endure.
For in this wild world where joy leaves its mark,
The heart learns to dance, and the soul learns to spark.

The Last Light of Day

In the garden, shadows play,
As the sun goes down to sway,
The daisies giggle, oh so bright,
While the roses blush, in twilight's light.

Bees buzz round with silly grace,
Bumping leaves, a clumsy race,
Even here, the crickets chime,
With a tune lost in time.

But oh! That buttercup so bold,
Tells secrets that can't be told,
Whispering jokes to the moon,
As if the stars are laughing too soon.

As day takes its final bow,
Who knew flowers could talk, somehow?
The last light shines with a grin,
And all the petals dance, let's begin!

Grief's Embrace in Bloom

In a pot, a cactus sighs,
Wishing for some sunny skies,
But what does it do all day?
Just pokes fun in its own way.

The ferns have formed a little band,
Playing tunes by nature's hand,
But one fell down, and oh, what fun!
A jovial laugh, "We've just begun!"

Tulips giggle in the breeze,
Telling tales with perfect ease,
While daisies snicker at the sun,
Their bright petals a moment's pun.

So let's toast with snail's slow crawl,
Amidst the blooms, we're having a ball,
In this garden, laughter reigns,
While nature winks at silly pains!

Petals Fall Like Tears

Petals drift like lost balloons,
Floating down to jaunty tunes,
"Catch me if you can!" they shout,
While bees are buzzing all about.

Oh, the daisies laugh aloud,
Beneath their little flower crowd,
"Don't be sad, just take a spin,
We'll dance in circles 'til we win!"

The violets play peek-a-boo,
Hiding in the grass so blue,
When the wind gives a hearty blow,
They tumble down in a gentle flow.

But even as the petals fall,
The sunshine's here to warm us all,
So giggle through the gentle breeze,
For every tear brings joyful tease!

Navigating Stillness

In silence sits a clever sprout,
Thinking deep without a doubt,
How do flowers find their way?
With great humor, they will sway.

The mossy rocks begin to chuckle,
Each ripple sounds a gentle snuggle,
While snails cruise at their own pace,
Trading stories in a race.

Petunia ponders, "What's the fuss?"
As breezes stir a subtle fuss,
"Let's make a joke of every stall,
And float like petals, after all!"

So when the world feels still and stuck,
Just giggle at your cleric luck,
For life in blooms takes gallant turns,
Where every laugh, a lesson earns!

Echoes of a Fragile Heart

In a garden where hopes grow fine,
A flower giggles, it's nearly time.
With petals painted in hues so bright,
She trips on dew and takes flight.

The bees all chuckle, buzzing away,
As the stem gets tangled in a ballet.
"Oh dear! Watch out for the wayward breeze!"
Yells the snail, while munching his peas.

A butterfly flutters, doing a dance,
While the lilypad dreams of romance.
But her jokes get twisted like vines on a fence,
And she resigns with a sigh of suspense.

So here's to the blooms with delicate grace,
Who stumble and trip through this silly race.
In every fall, there's laughter to find,
With echoes ringing through the mind.

Beneath the Weeping Willow

Beneath a tree with branches wide,
A squirrel scurries, full of pride.
He trips on roots and falls in a heap,
Wondering where his acorns sleep.

The wind whispers tales of the foolish cat,
Who thought she could pounce, but got stuck in a spat.
With a flip and a flop, she takes to the air,
Landing right down in a patch of despair.

A rabbit hops in, with a twitch and a grin,
He claims he can dance, but it's quite a spin.
With thumps and thuds, he breaks from the beat,
And we all laugh at his clumsy retreat.

So gathered we are, beneath branches long,
Sharing our blunders in a whimsical song.
For each little fumble, each flip of the tail,
Turns into laughter, a glorious tale.

A Song of Frayed Edges

In a garden where threads intertwine,
A seamstress sighs, looking for wine.
Her stitches are crooked, her fabric a mess,
While daisies smirk in their floral dress.

Her thimble escapes like a runaway star,
Rolling on the floor, traveling far.
"Oh, come back!" she calls, with a theatrical flair,
As the cat plots to pilot it high through the air.

The spools of ribbon tangle in knots,
As she crafts a gown fit for elegant thoughts.
But with each twist, her designs start to creep,
And end up a dress that's not hers to keep.

Yet laughter weaves through each silly mishap,
Creating a fabric adorned with a clap.
So let the threads fray, let the seams break,
For joy can be found in the paths that we make.

The Tides of Twilight

At twilight's call, the waves dance in glee,
While crabs do their cha-cha, as bold as can be.
With shells as their hats, they strut on the shore,
Counting their steps, but forgetting the score.

A seagull swoops by with a taco to munch,
While a fish jumps up, trying to bunch.
"Hey, keep it down!" says the clam with a shout,
As he scribbles in sand, mapping his route.

The starfish spin tales of treasures untold,
While the setting sun drapes the world in gold.
But the waves, they just giggle and crest,
Washing away plans, in their playful jest.

So let's raise a toast to the ocean's delight,
Where laughter and foolishness dance in the night.
For in every wave and each glimmering tide,
Humor awaits, where the sillies abide.

The Fragile Heart of Spring

In springtime blooms a heart so fine,
A petal swoops, oh what a sign!
It flutters here, it flutters there,
And sneezes pollen on the air.

A dandelion gives a wink,
While tulips giggle, what do you think?
They share their tales of winter's frown,
While busy bees buzz all around.

But watch your step, dear clumsy friend,
The fragile heart may just descend!
With a comical plop it lands,
In muddy fields, not where it planned.

So take a breath and do not fret,
For springtime's laughs we won't forget!
With giggles shared in flowered cheer,
The heart of spring is always near.

Solitude Beneath the Blossoms

Beneath the blooms, where shadows creep,
A quirky critter dares to leap.
He finds a spot, quite cozy too,
To nap and dream in pink and blue.

The wind whispers secrets, silly and sweet,
While birds practice their tap dance feat.
But wait! A sneeze that breaks the calm,
A wayward pollen brings no harm.

The butterfly giggles, what a burst!
As petals rain down, it's a flower first!
In solitude's cradle, laughter is loud,
While blossoms sway, oh how they proud!

The blooms are shy, yet they all conspire,
To entertain a heart's desire.
For solitude, with blossoms near,
Is a funny place, that's quite clear!

The Dance of Dusk and Dew

At dusk, the flowers find their groove,
With twirls and twists, they start to move.
Dewdrops laugh as they leap and spin,
In a dampened dance, they always win!

Fairies giggle, brush their hair,
While petals float on evening air.
A moonbeam steps in with a wink,
And whispers secrets not a soul would think.

The breeze carries a ticklish tease,
As petals sway with utmost ease.
While crickets play a soft serenade,
The earth itself begins to fade.

With every whirl and every sway,
The flowers laugh at the end of day.
Dusk and dew, a sight so bright,
In their silly dance, they find delight!

Secrets in the Marsh

In the marshy lands where secrets hide,
A toad wears boots, with too much pride.
He hops and skips through mud and muck,
While teasing frogs about their luck.

The cattails whisper, 'What a show!'
As wiggly worms put on a tow.
With goofy grins, they all parade,
In a wobbly line, no masquerade.

A dragonfly zooms without a care,
And sends a splash, oh what a scare!
The marsh erupts in chuckles deep,
As secrets hidden cannot keep.

In silliness wrapped in swampy glee,
The whispers of humor flow like a spree.
In the marsh, where laughter's found,
The secrets spill, joy unbound.

Whispers of the Water's Edge

At the water's edge, I spy a frog,
Hopping wildly, with a wink and a jog,
He croaks a tune, so silly and bright,
While dragonflies dance in the fading light.

The fish all giggle, they splash and they swirl,
As I trip on a rock and give it a whirl,
My hat flies off, an unfortunate scene,
The frogs all laugh, 'What a fine routine!'

In the reeds, there's mischief, a hidden delight,
With turtles and crickets plotting all night,
They scheme for a race, oh who will be bold?
It's a laughter-filled world, bright green and gold.

So remember, dear friend, as you wander and play,
Life's full of laughter in the silliest way,
Join in the joy, let your worries take flight,
At the water's edge, everything feels right.

Petals in Shadows

In the garden's shade, a petal confesses,
With colors so bright, yet awkwardly dresses,
It sways with a giggle, whispering low,
'Why do the bees always steal the show?'

A butterfly flutters, and tries a new pose,
But stumbles in dance, as the flower just glows,
They laugh at the breeze that tousles their hair,
In this petal-filled theater, shenanigans flare.

The daisies join in, they twist and they twirl,
Swaying to rhythms that make the bees whirl,
A sunflower chuckles, its seeds just a show,
Saying, 'I'm the tallest, just thought you should know!'

So when life feels heavy, and shadows grow long,
Remember the petals, who sing their own song,
In laughter and light, they find their own way,
Turning each moment to a whimsical play.

The Silent Cry of Bloom

A bud peeked out, with a quizzical frown,
Why do we bloom just to nap on the ground?
The sun's beam tickles, but oh what a tease,
As ants march and dance, saying, 'Do as you please!'

With petals outstretched, it tried to have fun,
Yet wind played a trick, and off it had run,
It tumbled and giggled, rolling in glee,
Saying, 'Who needs elegance? Look at me!'

The daisies looked on with delightful surprise,
At this mischievous bloom, a joy in disguise,
Together they chuckled, 'The world's quite absurd,'
In the garden of laughter, not a voice heard.

As blossoms burst forth, a wild little spree,
The blooms let out giggles, a bright tapestry,
So if you get caught in the stillness of boom,
Join in the laughter at the silent bloom.

Fragments of a Withered Dream

In a corner forgotten, a dream lay in wait,
With petals all crinkled, it whispered of fate,
'I once was so vivid, with colors so bold,
Now look at me here, like a story retold.'

It chuckles to find, the world keeps on spinning,
While the weeds nearby, oh, they keep on grinning,
A dandelion laughs, with its fuzzy bold mane,
'Look at us, friend, we're winning the game!'

The clock ticks just right, as the sunlight goes down,
A puff of wind blows, and it spins like a crown,
So even when wilting, there's humor in seams,
Fragments of laughter live deep in our dreams.

So raise up your voice, let the giggles be heard,
In the face of the wilt, let joy be preferred,
For even in withering, there's magic in sight,
In fragments of dreams, we'll dance through the night.

A Bloom Under Moonlight

In the garden, blooms so bright,
Crickets chirp in the night.
A flower winks with a twist,
Says, "Hey there! Don't you miss?"

Dancing shadows, quite the sight,
Petals giggle, pure delight.
A bee buzzes, does a spin,
Sipping nectar, grinning wide with a grin.

A breeze whispers a silly tale,
Of mischievous snails on the trail.
They slide and glide, oh what a farce,
Leaving trails like silly sparse.

As moonlight spills on the ground,
Flowers dream without a sound.
In laughter, they bloom and sway,
Underneath the stars so gay.

The Serenade of Soft Petals

Petals plucked in the sun's bright glow,
Strumming tunes, putting on a show.
Pansies laugh, their voices sweet,
While daisies dance on tiny feet.

A bumblebee joins in the choir,
Buzzing notes that never tire.
With a wink, a tulip sways,
Joking over sunny days.

In a breeze, the petals flap,
As if caught in a playful trap.
Nonsense blooms where flowers play,
Silly games throughout the day.

At dusk, the laughter finds its rest,
Petals yawn, they've done their best.
A soft hush over blooms falls,
As night softly whispers its calls.

Elegy of the Quiet Pond

The pond reflects a frog's old croak,
Ribbiting songs, a froggy joke.
Water lilies float with grace,
In their stillness, a happy face.

Dragonflies dance, a buzzing spree,
Whirling around, so wild and free.
A heron stands, poised for a catch,
Yet slips and lands with a panicked scratch.

Reeds sway as the wind plays near,
Whispering secrets only they hear.
The fish below giggle and glide,
Watching antics from their watery hide.

At twilight, the ripples fade,
With chuckles shared, they serenade.
The pond, a stage for nature's jest,
Where laughter lingers, never rests.

Reflections on a Gentle Breeze

A gentle breeze tickles leaves,
Making tiny whispers weave.
Clouds drift lazily in the sky,
Chasing butterflies that flit by.

The sunlight dances on the path,
Lighting up the flowers' laugh.
Tulips wink with a colors' swirl,
While daisies twirl in a floral whirl.

Squirrels chuckle up in trees,
Juggling acorns with such ease.
A playful gust sways the scene,
Bringing joy, bright and keen.

As shadows lengthen in the light,
The world holds its breath at night.
But in dreams, the blooms will tease,
Still laughing softly on the breeze.

Cradled by the Twilight

As twilight wrapped me like a shawl,
I tripped on shadows, took a fall.
The fireflies winked, quite mischievous,
While I laughed loud, feeling ridiculous.

The stars peeked through, a cheeky grin,
I danced alone, just me and my chin.
The grass tickled my toes in delight,
As I swayed, oh what a sight!

The moon laughed low, a soft big belly,
While I juggled dreams, shaky and jelly.
A bird chirped out a snarky tune,
With giggles echoing under the moon!

In the cradle of dark, we all conspire,
To be silly fools, the fun doesn't tire.
Each laugh a spark in twilight's embrace,
Old dusk and I, a comical chase!

The Ghost of a Moonlit Evening

A phantom floated by with a wig,
Wobbling awkwardly, looking quite big.
It mumbled like it lost its own cue,
Wishing for laughs, not just boo-hoo.

With every shimmer of silver light,
It twirled through the air, a comical sight.
It tripped on clouds, fell flat on its butt,
Then giggled out loud, 'Is this really what?'

The trees whispered jokes in hushed tones,
As giggles filled gardens, shaking old stones.
The ghost just chuckled, a jolly old chap,
Making the night a whimsical nap.

In shadows and beams, we all shared a jest,
Who knew eerie times could be such a fest?
With every giggle, the spirits took flight,
Enjoying the quirks of a moonlit night!

Fragments of a Faded Memory

In a scrapbook of giggles, I once found,
A snapshot of me making silly sounds.
With my hair in pigtails, I wore a grin,
In a world where the nutty is always in.

The memories played hide-and-seek,
With old teddy bears that humorously squeak.
I remember the time I got stuck in a chair,
And everyone laughed at my floppy despair.

Each fragment rekindles a joy so bright,
Like bubbles of laughter that take flight.
With sprinkles of charm and a dash of fun,
I sailed through the year, my smiles were spun.

In this fade of time, I find delight,
In each little twist, from morning to night.
With every chuckle, the past comes alive,
A whimsical dance that helps us all thrive!

The Weight of Wistful Wishes

Wishes piled high, a humorous mess,
A mountain of hopes, I must confess.
I wished for a cat, but got a dog,
Who pranced around like a silly fog.

Each whimsy twinkled like stars in my eyes,
While my dreams floated out, oh my, what a surprise!
To ride on a cloud, or so I had thought,
Instead, I was left in a tangled knot.

With the weight of my dreams, I giggled aloud,
As I stumbled through life with an unkempt crowd.
Wistful wishes turned into bright jokes,
Where laughter reigns, and humor invokes.

The burden of longing is lightened with glee,
For every odd wishing bone sets me free.
What once was a woe, is now a grand show,
In the weight of my wishes, I follow the flow!

When Colors Fade to Gray

Bright flowers bloom in a sunny spree,
But one little petal was lost at sea.
Hiding from sunshine, it lost its way,
Now pouting in corners, all gritty and gray.

Rabbits chuckle, while squirrels invade,
Mocking the flower, now stuck in the shade.
"Stop sulking, dear petal, embrace the frost!"
But it just shivers, feeling so lost.

Ladybugs giggle, as bees start to tease,
"Come join the party, shake off your freeze!"
But the petal just huffs, a dramatic scene,
Pretending it's royalty, so quiet, so keen.

With a sigh and a shimmer, it gleams with flair,
Deciding that gray could use some repair.
It danced with the shadows, a triumphant sway,
Who knew frowns could turn to a beautiful day!

The Pulse of Nature's Tears

Rainclouds grumble, with brows tightly furrowed,
A moody sky that's thoroughly borrowed.
Droplets splatter on flowers too proud,
"Quit your whining!" they yell to the cloud.

Puddles form laughter, all splashes and dance,
While thorns roll their eyes at the wet circumstance.
Trees shake their leaves, those naughty little spies,
"Get over yourself, you're just in disguise!"

A drop on a petal, what shall it do?
It wobbles and wobbles, then bids adieu.
"Farewell, my friends, I'm off to the brook!"
With a splash and a giggle, it snuck like a crook.

Nature's a stage, with tears turned to cheer,
Each sob brings mischief, each curve brings near.
So if you find clouds with their frowns, you've seen,
Just wait for the rainbow, it'll giggle between!

Drowned in Reflection

A pond so serene, a glassy facade,
Holding secrets of frogs who are quite the charade.
Ripples of laughter disrupt the calm plight,
As fish start to giggle at their own silly sight.

A quacker approaches, with a splash in the air,
"Why are we swimming?" she gasps with a stare.
But fish twist and twirl, with fins fluttering fast,
"Life's just a splash, don't let it slip past!"

They see their reflections, and what do they see?
A frog in a tutu? A fish on a spree?
They split into fits of unbridled delight,
While waves carry giggles, a wonderful sight.

So here in the depths, they float and they play,
Finding joy in the moments, come dance in the spray.
Who knew underwater could bring such a cheer,
Just a twist of fate, it's their favorite sphere!

Silence of the Water's Edge

At the water's edge, where the stillness spills,
Lies a frog with ambitions and lots of big thrills.
"I shall be a prince!" it croaks with great flair,
While ducks just roll eyes, as they ponder his hair.

Crickets chirp softly, they giggle and stare,
"Oh frog, your ambitions are beyond compare!"
With bulging vision, and a grand little grin,
He leaps with such hope, with splashes akin.

Then the water ripples and ripples some more,
While the frog strikes a pose, now he's back on the shore.

"Why wish to be royal, when a jester's the key?"
He twirls with delight, a joke, can't you see?

So the edges stay lively with whispers and play,
Where dreams become laughter and hopes float away.
In the silence of water, joy reigns like a jest,
The prince of the pond simply needs a good rest!

Beneath a Veil of Petals

Under a canopy, soft and bright,
Dancing around, a silly sight.
Petals tumble, like little clowns,
Painting the grass in whimsical gowns.

Bouncing bees with mischief to share,
Tickle the blooms, without a care.
The sun chuckles, a warm embrace,
As flowers giggle in their own space.

A breeze comes by, and they all sway,
Flirting with raindrops that wish to play.
With every flutter, there's laughter mixed,
The garden stirs, a joy so fixed.

But when the dusk wraps its cloak tight,
The petals whisper secrets at night.
They dream of joy, beneath stars' beams,
In a world where nothing's as it seems.

The Melancholy of Green Leaves

Green leaves sigh with a playful twist,
Grumbling about the sun they missed.
Hoping for rain, a gloomy wish,
Yet laughing deep in a swaying swish.

A caterpillar, dressed for the ball,
Wants to be big, but is feeling small.
He trips on a twig, then shrugs with glee,
'These leaves are mine; I'm fancy and free!'

When lightning strikes a fit of laughter,
The leaves jump high, their follow-up after.
They chatter loudly when winds do scream,
In this leafy world, they live the dream.

Yet as night falls, they quietly scheme,
Planning mischief, or so it seems.
With dreams of fun, and a party vast,
Tomorrow's light will make memories last.

Aroma of Forgotten Dreams

In the garden, scents swirl and twirl,
Whispering secrets in a fragrant whirl.
Pansies giggle, their perfume bright,
While daisies plot mischief in pure delight.

Old roses mumble, their stories grand,
Of lovesick bees and the pollen band.
But lilacs laugh at the grand old tales,
With petals grinning, they don't need scales.

A whiff of nostalgia brings smiles anew,
As chubby bunnies munch on morning dew.
While dandelions, wild and free,
Wish for adventure, a grand jubilee.

With each breeze that carries their cheer,
The air is alive with giggles sincere.
Though dreams may fade as the day drifts cold,
In scents of laughter, their tales unfold.

A Sigh Among the Reeds

Amidst tall reeds, a froggy squeaks,
Hopping along while the river creeks.
With every leap, a chuckle escapes,
As dragonflies chase in funny shapes.

The reeds sway gently, arms open wide,
Trying to catch the wind's playful ride.
They gossip softly, sharing their woes,
Of muddy water and pesky crows.

A fish pops up with a splashy grin,
Joining the antics, let the fun begin!
The sun dips low, the shadows entwine,
As laughter echoes, all is just fine.

But with twilight's hush, the jokes grow thin,
And even frogs yawn, tired of the din.
Yet in the reeds, a promise remains,
Tomorrow's antics will dance in their veins.

Beneath a Sky of Fading Dreams.

In a garden where shadows dance,
A flower tried to take a chance.
With petals wide and dreams so bright,
She tripped on roots, what a silly sight!

She whispered soft to the buzzing bees,
'Oh, can't you see? I'm built for ease!'
But they just laughed, took her for a spin,
And off she flew on a gusty wind.

Whispers of the Water Lily

On the pond, she's floating free,
Nattily dressed for a tea party!
But when she sways with a gusty push,
Her hat goes flying; oh, what a rush!

The frogs croak loud, join in the fun,
'Your tea's a splash! Now don't you run!'
She laughed and spun, a sight to behold,
As pearls of laughter began to unfold.

Echoes in the Garden

The daisies chuckled, joined the show,
The tulips danced with quite a glow.
Our flower friend, with a sigh and a grin,
Said, 'Why don't we add some giggles to the din?'

A breeze swept through, they all took flight,
Tickling tongues and hearts so light.
'We're not just blooms,' they sang in chorus,
'We're jesters grand beneath the sun's glow-fur!'

Shadows on Still Waters

Reflecting laughter on the waves,
A lily joked, 'These are my caves!'
The ripples giggled, told her right,
'You're the queen of folly — what a sight!'

But just as she basked in her fame,
A fly buzzed by and called her name.
She ducked and dived, a splash and a splash,
Too busy laughing, to keep her stash!

A Tapestry of Desolation

In a garden where weeds make their dance,
A shoe lost its sole in a daring prance.
With crickets that chirp, a loud serenade,
The flowers all giggle, but the grass feels betrayed.

A butterfly lands with a tattered wing,
As if it forgot how to flutter and sing.
Dandelions scream as they burst into flight,
While daisies roll their eyes at this outrageous sight.

The sun wears a hat that's slightly askew,
As shadows stretch long, laughing at the view.
One petal's gone missing, oh where could it be?
A squirrel's pressed charges on a raucous bee.

And yet in this chaos, a charm settles down,
As blooms shed their worries and don silly crowns.
With laughter in petals and chuckles in dew,
This tapestry trembles in a giggled hue.

The Weight of Unopened Buds

In the hedge where the roses don't dare to bloom,
A cactus is plotting its plans of great doom.
With a sigh of the breeze, a dandelion yawns,
As bees take notes on the gossip in dawns.

The buds are just waiting, oh what a tease,
Practicing poses with whimsical ease.
One thinks it can dance, but it trips on a leaf,
And the tree laughs so hard, it's beyond all belief.

A snail in a shell claims to be quite profound,
While a worm in the earth is just stuck underground.
The azaleas whisper of parties ahead,
But the weight of unopened buds lingers instead.

Amidst all the banter and leafy charades,
The sun's lost its glasses, oh what a charade.
Yet each tiny creature, in chaos so sweet,
Finds joy in the wait – a silly retreat.

Whispers Beneath the Surface

In ponds where the frogs wear their best fuzzy hats,
A fish tells a tale that's riddled with spats.
With a wink to the lily, who tries hard to float,
The dragonflies chuckle, staying just out of coat.

The reeds hum a tune, slightly offbeat,
While turtles crack jokes that are hard to repeat.
Beneath the still waters, the laughter is bold,
As a crab shows the moves, quite daring and old.

Ripples of giggles weave tales through the night,
As fireflies join in, providing soft light.
A pair of sly otters, in mischief they swim,
Bathe in the moonlight, on a whim and a whim.

Yet deep down the pond, where no one can poke,
A wise old catfish gives a snort and a joke.
For in each little wave, a ripple of fun,
In whispers beneath, is the giggle of one.

Farewell to Vibrant Days

As autumn arrives with a clumsy twirl,
The leaves do a shuffle, give nature a whirl.
A squirrel in a turtleneck, sporting a grin,
Stocks up on acorns, for winter's thick skin.

The sun fumbles bright, with a blush and a smirk,
While shadows play tag, doing their quirky work.
With pumpkins all laughing in orange-hued glee,
They remind us of summers that once were so free.

The crickets serenade, a bittersweet tune,
As moonbeams forecast a bright harvest moon.
Yet each fading glow wears a festive disguise,
In the farewell of colors, humor still flies.

So wave to the daisies, and bid them adieu,
As winter creeps in with a cold fuzzy shoe.
For though vibrant days seem to drift far away,
In laughter we hold them, come what may.

Blooming in the Absence

In a garden where laughter blooms,
Colors dance among the fumes.
A daisy snickers at the rose,
Says, "You've never struck a pose!"

The tulip twirls, a goofy sight,
While violets giggle with delight.
"Who needs sunshine," they all cheer,
"When we've got this funny air here!"

A gnome grins wide, a friend to all,
Hiding behind the garden wall.
He whispers jokes to bumblebees,
Who buzz with laughter in the breeze.

For every petal that has fallen,
Jokes are shared, and laughter's callin'.
In absence, joy still finds a way,
Laughter brightens every day!

The Last Echo of the Meadow

In the meadow, where tall grass sways,
A chirpy bird sings silly praise.
"Did you hear the cow jump high?"
"Not as high as the pig can fly!"

Bubbles rise from a gopher's hole,
He's laughing hard, he's on a roll.
"Why do daisies wear such hats?"
"To avoid the laughter from the spats!"

As butterflies flit with graceful flair,
Each one knows without a care.
A snail slips past, says with a grin,
"Why be slow, when you can spin?"

Though echoes fade and shadows creep,
The jokes they shared forever leap.
In the meadow of joyous din,
Every giggle keeps us in!

Beneath the Veil of Mourning

In a park where sad hearts collide,
A squirrel jokes, with eyes wide.
"Why the long face on that tree?"
"He just lost his leaves, you see!"

A cactus sways, feeling quite sore,
"I'm prickly, but I still want more!"
The ferns nod, their wispy hair,
"Such drama here, we have to share!"

Despite the shade where shadows grow,
Laughter bubbles, it steals the show.
"Why did the droopy flower pout?"
"Because he hears the bees shout out!"

In mourning's veil, they play their part,
With silly tales to heal the heart.
For every petal lost in gloom,
Joy will surely find its room!

Between Bluebells and Heartache

In the field where bluebells ring,
A bird sneezed, what a thing!
Butterflies burst into laughter bright,
As flowers giggled, quite the sight.

A bumblebee with a funny buzz,
Tripped over grass and then because,
It tried to dance, oh what a fuss,
The rabbits chuckled, 'What a bus!'

Yet in the midst of bloom and jest,
A heartache whispered, 'This is best.'
But even sadness wore a grin,
In blooms so bold, joy creeps in.

So here we laugh, though tears may play,
Each flower sways, come what may.
In ruffled petals, joy's clear tune,
Life's quirks dance in the afternoon.

When the Sun Forgot to Shine

The sun woke late, a goofy gaffe,
Clouds chuckled hard, what a laugh!
Raindrops played on rooftops bright,
Splashing puddles with all their might.

A cat in a hat, strutting with style,
Gazed at the clouds and paused awhile.
With a flick of its tail, it jumped in surprise,
As a shadow blinked, oh my, what a prize!

The sun peeked out with a sheepish grin,
Shining through storms, with a twirl and spin.
But rain danced on, in puddles delight,
Even the sun found it hard not to bite.

So here's to days that dawdle and sway,
When sunshine plays hide-and-seek all day.
In laughter's embrace, let us collide,
For even dull moments can't hide our stride.

In the Presence of Fleeting Beauty

A butterfly flitted, all dressed in flair,
It winked at a flower, who said, 'How rare!'
They laughed so sweet, in the breeze's hold,
As petals whispered their secrets untold.

Yet time's a trickster, it wouldn't stay,
It tickled the bloom, then slipped away.
The flower sighed, 'Oh fleeting grace,
Why couldn't beauty just slow its pace?'

With a chuckle and twirl, the petals danced,
In a merry jig, they took their chance.
For even as beauty drifts with the day,
Joy lingers long where laughter can play.

So let us frolic in moments bright,
Chasing the smiles that spark our delight.
In the fleeting dance of beauty's cue,
Laughter unfurls, ever anew.

The Shadows Dance at Dusk

As shadows stretch with a playful sigh,
Nighttime whispers, 'Oh my, oh my!'
A squirrel juggles acorns, quite a feat,
While crickets cheer with a tap on their feet.

The moonwears a mask of a smiling grin,
As stars twinkle jokes that spark from within.
With the wind on its toes, a breeze swirled past,
Swaying the trees in a rhythm unsurpassed.

But just as the laughter reached its peak,
A bat flew by, doing a sneak!
With a flap and a flip, it gave us a fright,
In the silliness of dusk, the world felt right.

So here's to shadows that gracefully prance,
In the cool of the night, let's join the dance.
Embrace the giggles that dusk has sent,
In the joy of the evening, let our hearts be lent.

www.ingramcontent.com/pod-product-compliance
Lightning Source LLC
Chambersburg PA
CBHW071815160106
43209CB00003B/100